Fog

poems of loss and hope

Wil Michael Wrenn

Fog

2336 Tallaha Road
Tillatoba, MS 38961 USA

CelticPoet@gmx.com

Published by Prolific Pulse Press LLC
Published in Raleigh, North Carolina USA

ISBN   979-8-9875200-5-5 Paperback

Library of Congress Control Number: 2023903070

Other Books by Wil Michael Wrenn

Songs of Solitude

Seasons of a Sojourner

Enid Lake Mosaic

Dedication

I dedicate the following poems to those who have passed over, in the hope and belief that souls never die … and love never dies.

Acknowledgments

The poems "The Passing of a Friend (For Brenda),"
"Double Ceremony," "Cold Reunion, and ""Reminiscence"
are taken from the author's first book *Songs of Solitude.*
"Reminiscence" also appeared in the author's third book,
Enid Lake Mosaic, published by Silver Bow Publishing of
British Columbia, Canada.

The poem "The Death of Innocence" first appeared in *Vita
Brevis Poetry Magazine* where it won the Editor's Choice
award. It is taken from the author's second book, *Seasons
of a Sojourner*, published by Silver Bow Publishing.

The poem "Beyond the Door" is also taken from *Seasons of
a Sojourner*.

The prose poem "The Meeting" first appeared in the
literary journal *Teach. Write*.

The poems "Absence," "For Ralph," "Last Will and
Testament," "Fog," first appeared in the journal *Literary
Yard*.

Table of Contents

Fog

Fog

Fog

Ambulance Wail

Dark of night,

flash of light,

crash of car,

blood on the highway.

Body and spirit

torn apart.

Ambulance wail…

lifting of the veil

between this world

and the next.

The Passing of a Friend
(For Brenda)

Something touched me lightly on the face,
Showing me some lonely distant place.
Was it just the haunting wind
Or the spirit of a passing friend?
I still know that death is not the end.

Suddenly a Presence did appear
And said to me, "There is no need to fear;
She is safe, son, here with Me;
She is now completely free;
She has found her pathway to the sea."

Seems the day is brighter than before;
I can see her standing at the door,
Waiting...wanting to go in
To the Father once again;
Thus, the journey ends where it began.

My soul ascends as if to follow them—

Fog

Friends of mine who've gone to be with Him;
But human eyes can only sigh
When they look upward to the sky
And wonder what it's really like to fly.

Gliding there with silvery wings on high,
Looking down to see it's earthly tie,
"Live!" my saddened spirit cried
To my wounded mortal side--
But another friend of mine has died.

Now I know she's joined the rest of them;
My light, too, is growing ever dim.
If it should fade out some night
In the middle of my flight,
There'll still be a greater, guiding Light.

The passing of a friend has brought a tear;
The passing of a friend has left me here,
Feeling things that she will never feel,
For death is something time can never heal--
What is an illusion, what is real?

Fog

Double Ceremony

There you lie
With your hands on your lap...
So still, so silent, so cold,
Unlike days of old
When I knew you by your laughter.

Now above you the rafters ring,
Echo the sound of chapel bells...
And I just sit and stare,
Unaware they knell for me
As well as you.

Cold Reunion

On this late-October night

with the full moon shining bright,

here we are again –

reunited,

In a manner of speaking,

beneath the vastness

of star-filled skies

and a wide expanse of tall pines.

But the only thing left

to help me remember you

is a cold, gray, tombstone

at the head of your grave.

I wonder…

Are you any happier there

than you were here,

happier than I am now? —

I truly hope so.

Part of you

that once felt so warm

to my touch,

Fog

lies deep in the earth,

alone,

with eyes closed,

seeing, feeling nothing…

The cool, green grass growing

silently over you.

And I stand above

with my eyes open,

yet seeing, feeling nothing

(too benumbed to even think) …

The cool, green grass trampled

thoughtlessly under my feet.

There's an idea

that's very tempting to me

at this moment:

I could almost be persuaded

to join you there

if you could but tell me,

convince me that you are

indeed happier than before,

Fog

at peace and at rest –

But you cannot,

and thus I'll decline…

For the time being, anyway.

But why so somber?

I'll return… someday

to go where you have gone

(and far too soon, I know).

And until then,

I'll come here every day

to this place

where the green grass grows

cool and deep,

covering you

while you sleep,

and as the daylight ends

and the darkness descends

and the pines, like sentinels,

seem to close in,

while the night comes quickly

but quietly on,

Fog

in silence I'll stoop low

to lay fresh-picked flowers,

gently,

beside your stone.

Fog

The Death of Innocence

My father was a farmer
with a 10th grade education –
and a 150 IQ.
My mother was a housewife,
factory worker, and nurse's aide.

In the schools of today,
she would have been
a special education student
in math, although she was good
in language arts.

There was an innocence about my mother.
She believed in the right and the good.
She believed God would listen,
come to the rescue,
help and heal.

Bedridden and suffering intensely,
she asked God to do that.
And in her trusting innocence

she believed – as long as she could,
until she fell into semi-consciousness.

Fog

Was God there at the last?
Did she see or know?
Was she betrayed in her belief?
For me, these are questions
that will always remain.

All I know
is that I stood by feeling helpless,
praying, listening, waiting, wandering,
as I silently watched
the death of innocence.

Live Your Life
(On the Day of My Aunt's Burial)

We get lulled to sleep

by everyday life,

and we often forget

that the clock is ticking…

ticking…ticking our lives away.

We forget what's important –

loving our family and friends,

our pets and all creation,

doing good to others

and showing mercy.

Our time here

is but a drop of water

in the ocean of eternity,

a flash – and then we're gone.

So, don't put off an act

or a word of love, or solace,

Fog

or spending time with those
who mean the most to you.

They say we will all meet again
on the other side,
on that distant shore
when resurrection comes.

But between here and there,
between us and our loved ones
who have gone before,
there is a great chasm
that we cannot bridge –
that only God can bridge.

So, cherish life
and those you love
while you still can.

Don't get lulled to sleep
by the everyday,
because the clock is ticking…

Fog

ticking…ticking our lives away,
and time and life are fleeting.

So, while you are alive,
while there is still time –
live your life!

Fog

I Wish

I miss my daddy and mama.
I wish I could see them again;
I wish I could talk with them again
and just be near them.

I wish I could know where they are
and how they are doing.
I wish they could tell me;
I wish they could show me.

I cannot bridge the gulf between us;
I would have to die to do that,
but I wish God would bridge it
and let them communicate with me.

It's so lonely here without them –
our loved ones who have passed.
It is said that God knows all,
but does He know just how lonely we are?

I wish this reality could be different,

Fog

but sadly it is not.

So, all I have is just wishing –

wishing that I could see and talk

with my parents once again.

Fog

Fog

Reminiscence

The wind blows cold across the lake--
I think of you.
The chill seems to penetrate
straight to the very marrow
of my bones--
I remember you.
The crystal clear water,
like a giant mirror
lying on the surface of the earth,
reflects the slate blue sky above--
I picture you.
The trees catch the muted rays
of the sun...
The waves ripple...
The leaves rustle...
I divine your presence here--
wistfully.

Absence

Sometimes I think I hear
your footsteps, but I turn,
and you're not there.

Sometimes I think I hear
your voice calling out,
but then I wake from my dream.

Sometimes I think I hear
your laughter, but it's only
the sound that silence makes.

Sometimes I think I hear
you whispering softly to me,
but it's only the echo of the wind.

Sometimes I seem to feel
your presence here with me,
but all that's really left

is just a poignant memory…
a haunting, wistful memory.

When Death Comes

When we take our last breath,

breathing in and breathing out,

are we then somewhere else,

conscious, aware,

with our loved ones again

never to say good-bye again –

is that what happens

when death comes?

Do we step out of fog

and into radiant light –

the light of life eternal?

We must wait until we see --

when death comes.

Fog

The Meeting

I had not seen her or heard from her
for a very long time. I did not know
where she was or how she was. Then
one cool, rainy day, just after dusk,
my phone rang. I answered it, and immediately
I recognized her voice. I was greatly surprised,
and I didn't know how she got my number,
as I had changed to a private number long since.
She requested to see me, and I was even
more surprised. She wanted me to meet her
at midnight at the beach house where we once
spent many wonderful, happy hours. I prepared
for my trip with anxiety and impatience, wanting
very much to see her but wondering why
after all this time she wanted to see me.
The clock slowly ticked the time by,
and I finally started on my journey.
I put in some music that we both loved
and had often listened to. All along the way,

Fog

I kept wondering what all of this meant,

why she had contacted me and wanted to see me

after all this time. Finally, I arrived at the beach house;

it and the beach were as lovely as I remembered.

I walked down to the beach. The rain had stopped,

but a fog had settled in, giving the entire area

an eerie look and feel.

Suddenly, I heard someone call my name.

I turned around, and there she was,

coming toward me, and wearing the most beautiful

white dress, long and flowing. How unusual,

I thought, for a meeting at the beach.

As she came near to me, the years, sadness,

and loneliness melted away. We spent the next

few hours walking along the beach, talking,

reminiscing, remembering, and forgetting.

We held each other close, again and again,

and I told her how much I had missed her,

and how I didn't understand her leaving.

She cried, said she had her reasons,

Fog

some even she herself didn't understand.
About an hour before sunrise, she said
she had to go. I told her I wanted to see her again,
and she told me she would see me soon.
She said she needed some time alone, so
I left her there, walked back to my car,
and started to drive away. I looked back,
and the last time I saw her, she was standing
on the beach looking out over the dark water,
she in her long, white, flowing dress,
shrouded by the fog.

As I drove home filled with happiness and sadness,
I wondered about our meeting and what it meant.
When I got home, I turned on the television,
fixed a cup of hot cocoa, and sat down to relax
a few minutes before trying to get some sleep.
I took a few sips, leaned back, and closed my eyes.
Suddenly, a voice from the television caused me
to sit up straight in my chair. This is what the voice said:

Fog

"Shortly before dusk today, the internationally known
artist Ariel's plane went down in a wooded area
a few miles from the coast. She was killed instantly."
I dropped my cup and stared at the television in disbelief.
My Ariel, with whom I had just spent hours
at our beach house and walking on the beach,
had come to see me one last time.
I was never the same after she left the first time.
I would never be the same after she left
for the last time. Changed forever -- both of us.
But I remembered her last words to me: "I'll see you soon."
And I have held on to that, even though
I could not hold on to her.

The Shadows and the Fog

We are afraid
of what is lurking in the shadows,
of what is hiding in the fog.
We had rather look from afar
at the shadows and the fog.

But what if we entered in
and then encountered there
those who had long since departed,
and what if we communed with them
and they also with us?

Would it have been worth it then,
despite our hesitation
and despite our trepidation,
for us to have entered in
to the shadows and the fog?

Fog

For Billy P.

I could never write about you;

for some reason,

when I thought of you

and what happened to you,

the words would not come.

You were a star athlete,

and I idolized you,

from the time we played

Little League baseball together

up through high school baseball.

You were a couple of grades

ahead of me in school,

but you were always kind and helpful,

building up a scrawny, younger kid

when you did not have to.

You had a bad car wreck

after you graduated,

Fog

and you were never the same again;
you would never completely regain
the health you had before.

The last time I ever saw you,
we played basketball on the court
of the First Baptist Church;
on that day, you bragged on me
one more time, one last time.

That was in the spring of '77;
you disappeared later that summer,
the summer Elvis died.
There were rumors swirling about you,
but no one knew what happened.

Months later in winter,
a hunter found your remains
and a gun on a creek bank
deep down in the woods
south of our little town.

Fog

I heard it rumored
that you left a note,
a last plaintive note,
and in it you said,
"I'm going to join the butterflies."

I hope you are indeed
as free now as a butterfly,
that somewhere beyond the sky
you are flying, oh, so high,
at peace -- at long last.

You were kind to me
and you will always be
alive in my memory,
and I'm glad I'm finally able
to write these words for you.

What happened was a tragedy,
one I'll never forget,
just as I won't forget you.

Fog

This is my tribute to you, Billy P.,
and I hope to see you again –

someday.

Fog

For Ralph

You were not a big kid,

and you didn't play sports,

but you were book smart.

You had diabetes

from your childhood,

and it got a lot worse

as the years went by.

Near the end,

when they told you

that you would go blind

and lose a limb,

you refused further treatment.

You died young,

but I hardly ever knew anyone

more full of life

and more courageous.

You were my friend,

and when my life is over,

I believe we'll meet again.

Fog

Vanished

It seems the older I get

the faster time flees.

Many of those I love

have already passed over,

and it won't be long

till I'll join them there.

Even if I live

to a ripe old age,

my time will come

all too soon.

In the blink of an eye

a decade passes,

and then two, and three.

I look in the mirror

and barely recognize

the old man there

looking back at me.

Fog

Old age creeped up on me,

but it seemed to happen

oh, so suddenly.

Our lives are a puff of smoke

carried away by the wind,

gone, never to return,

vanished …

to be no more.

So Much Wasted Time

You look up,

and the time is gone --

so much wasted time.

Too much said and done,

or not enough,

the chance to make up

for all of it

has long since passed

because the time is near

when you won't be here

any longer, or ever again.

Your life is like a flower

that bloomed for an hour

then cut down and decayed.

So much wasted time,

and no time left

to make things right;

Fog

you will soon be gone

and out of sight

of everyone here,

forgotten by most,

and mourned by few,

crossed over,

never to return …

so much wasted time.

Fog

Fog

Last Will and Testament

When my time has come

to leave this place,

just bury me in a plywood coffin,

or, better yet,

wrap me in a blanket

and bury me quickly,

without a funeral

or any memorial service.

I would not want anyone

to visit me after I'm dead

who could not come to see me

while I was among the living.

Maybe someone will care enough

to tend my grave,

to put some flowers there,

and remember me always.

If I could just have that,

it would be enough.

Fog

Beyond the Door

They sleep beneath the soil,
oblivious to the struggles
of those of us
who walk above them.

They know not pain anymore;
they have passed
through the door.

They know not the trials
and troubles of mortals,
the labors and cares
of the flesh.

Oblivious to strife,
they have gone
where sorrow cannot touch them,
at rest in the arms of God,
while we who remain
can only see with clouded eyes
in a dim light.

Fog

So, we stumble half-blind
through our lonely days
oblivious to life,
waiting for the moment
when we will join them –
those who have gone before,
beyond the door.

Fog

One-eyed Cat

He was just an old cat;
so what if he died;
he was only one-eyed --
I still cried.

Fog

My Beloved Pets

My beloved pets

have all passed over;

I could not hold them here,

but they remain in my memory

and in my heart.

The love they gave me

still lives within me;

they showed me

that there is indeed

such a thing

as unconditional love.

As long as I live,

I'll never forget them,

and they will abide with me.

Fog

Thoroughbreds

I've always been enchanted by
and drawn to thoroughbred racehorses.
My favorites were Seattle Slew and
his offspring Swale and Landaluce.

Then there were Seabiscuit and Secretariat,
and, most recently, Barbaro –
oh, how tragic was Barbaro's story,
and yet triumphant and heroic, too.

These horses are all gone now,
but they gave me pure joy
to see them run with such abandon.

In my imagination,
I see them running still
through misty hollows,
green fields and pastures,
feet barely touching the ground,
gliding almost on air
as they gallop along.

In my mind,

Fog

I can see them emerge

out of the mist and the fog

to run free forever

on the other side of that Bridge.

Fog

C

Communion of Saints

I have believed in the "communion of saints"
but though I commune with them,
I have no evidence
that they commune with me.

How ardently
do I desire to know
where my departed loved ones are,
to know that they are conscious,
thinking, feeling – alive somewhere.

I ask over and over again
why they cannot communicate with us.
That would ease the bereavement
of losing them.

I commune with them every day,
but they do not commune with me –
at least, I am unaware if they do.

Fog

Why won't God allow them
to contact those of us
still marooned here
on this island in the ocean
of infinity?

Surely He must know
how lonely we are,
how we hurt and grieve.

I guess that is our lot here –
to hope for and believe
in the communion of saints,
to earnestly yearn for it –
to commune with our beloved departed
and only wish for something,
for anything in return.

Fog

Fog

Fog

I like to walk at night
when the moon is full,
the fog has rolled in
and settled in the fields and hollows.

As I walk in moonlight and fog,
the boundary between this world
and the next seems fragile, thin;
what is real and what is imaginary
becomes blurred, obscured.

If I stand very still,
I can almost hear voices
of loved ones who have passed over.
I think I can hear
footsteps approaching and passing near.

I think I can see
ghostly figures moving through the fog,
moonlight illuminating their presence.

Fog

Fog envelops like a blanket,

making me want to remain here

in this place between reality and fantasy,

between the mundane and mystical,

between the physical and spiritual.

I can linger but cannot stay,

but I'll return to this realm

and commune with those beloved souls

when I walk again at night

in the luminous moonlight

and in the fog.

Author Profile

Wil Michael Wrenn was born in Charleston, MS, USA. He has traveled across the United States and resided in several places, but he currently lives in the hills of eastern Tallahatchie County near Charleston which he considers home. He has a special feeling for the hills, hollows, and landscape of North Mississippi. He is especially fond of Enid Lake which he considers to be one of the most beautiful, tranquil places he has ever seen. It has inspired many poems.

He has been writing since the age of twelve, first writing poems and then later lyrics and music. He bought a Sears guitar at age fifteen and taught himself to play it.

Since then he has written hundreds of poems and songs and had poems published in national and international anthologies and in magazines. He has also published three books of original poetry:

Songs of Solitude; Seasons of a Sojourner; and Enid Lake Mosaic; the latter two books were published by Silver Bow Publishing, of British Columbia, Canada.

Wil Michael is a songwriter-member and publisher-member of the American Society of Composers, Authors, and Publishers (ASCAP), a national performing rights organization for songwriters and publishers. His music publishing company is called Autumn Fields Publications. His website is: michaelwrenn.webstarts.com/

When not writing, playing music, singing, or teaching, he enjoys family and friends, reading good books, movies, travel, listening to good music, sports, spirituality, and just being out in nature.

Fog

Thank you for reading this collection of poetry.

If you would like to leave a review, it would be much appreciated.